Original title:
Calm Awakenings

Copyright © 2024 Book Fairy Publishing
All rights reserved.

Editor: Theodor Taimla
Author: Regiina Rannaveer
ISBN HARDBACK: 978-9916-759-78-3
ISBN PAPERBACK: 978-9916-759-79-0

Muted Morn

In the soft embrace of dawn,
Whispers of the night are gone.
Silence wears a golden hue,
Morning wakes the world anew.

Stillness dances with the breeze,
Songs of birds adorn the trees.
Skies unfurl like painted dreams,
Muted moments flow in streams.

Gentle Newness

Softly breaks the morning light,
Banishing the shades of night.
Glistening dew on petals rest,
Nature's calm in dawn expressed.

Tender hues of day's first glow,
Paint the world in a gentle flow.
Whispers of a brand-new day,
In the softest light of May.

Hushed Expanse

Vast horizons greet the day,
In a quiet, tender way.
Waves of amber, fields of gold,
Morning whispers, truths untold.

Silent echoes stretch afar,
Underneath the fading star.
Hushed expanse, a canvas wide,
Nature's beauty deified.

Day's First Light

Day breaks softly through the veil,
Morning's breath begins to sail.
Golden beams in silence spread,
Kissing dreams that gently fled.

Morn's embrace, so calm and bright,
Chasing away the shadowed night.
With each ray, hope starts to rise,
Painting hues in open skies.

Serenity Unfolded

Beneath the skies, where silence roams,
Whispering winds embrace the sea.
In tranquil waves, with gentle combs,
Serenity unfolds in glee.

The twilight drapes a silken hue,
Stars ignite the velvet night.
A peaceful calm, a world anew,
Dreams take flight in pure delight.

Mountains stand with stoic grace,
Rivers flow with soft refrain.
Nature's symphony, a tender embrace,
Echoes through the verdant plain.

Silent Renewal

In the dawn, the world awakes,
Birdsong weaves through morning air.
A quiet renewal, when night breaks,
Nature's charm, beyond compare.

Leaves whisper secrets of the past,
Roots embrace the earth so deep.
Life's cycle turns, never fast,
Awakening from winter's sleep.

Sunlight filters through the green,
Petals open, soft and bright.
In the silence, life unseen,
Renewal's glow in morning light.

Ethereal Beginnings

Where dreams take root, and stars align,
Ethereal mists cloak the dawn.
A realm between, so richly fine,
The night departs; new life is drawn.

Clouds drift across a painted sky,
Awakening an ancient song.
In stillness, whispers softly sigh,
A world where spirits dance along.

Moonlight fades, the sun arises,
Transforming shadows into light.
In every breath, new hope crystallizes,
Ethereal beginnings take flight.

Tranquil Transition

Golden fields sway in evening's glow,
A tranquil hush envelops all.
The sun dips low; the world's aglow,
As stars emerge, the night does call.

Shadows lengthen, whispers blend,
As twilight paints the sky serene.
In every breath, the colors fend,
Changing hues from gold to green.

The day surrenders to the night,
A quiet peace, a gentle yield.
In twilight's arms, a soft respite,
A transition, dreamlike and healed.

Dawn's Subtle Kiss

In the blush of morning, so tender and sweet,
A whisper of light where sky and earth meet.
Hues of pink and gold, a resplendent array,
Dawn's subtle kiss heralds the new day.

Glimmers of hope in each dew-laden blade,
Silent symphonies in the cool, gentle shade.
Every waking heartbeat, a promise reborn,
In the embrace of dawn, all sorrows are shorn.

Serene Lift

Gentle winds carry whispers of calm,
Serene lift beneath the old oaken palm.
Birdsongs cascading through soft, azure skies,
Peace in each note, a soulful disguise.

Ripples in the pond, reflections so clear,
Moments of tranquility, leaving us near.
To the quietude found in a silent drift,
In nature's tender embrace, our spirits lift.

Sundrenched Silence

Golden beams pour through the leafy canopy,
Sundrenched silence, a moment of clarity.
The world's hushed hum, beneath a radiant glow,
Time slows its march, in the afterglow.

Shadows play games on the sunlit floor,
Echoes of laughter we've heard before.
In this quiet interlude, hearts softly sing,
A symphony of silence in each sun-kissed thing.

Lucid Beginnings

First light kisses the horizon's edge,
Lucid beginnings from night's fleeting pledge.
A new script unfurling, in dawn's early pen,
Whispers of hope in each moment's zen.

Footsteps on paths yet untraveled, unseen,
The promise of dreams in sunrise's sheen.
In the bloom of morning, with colors so bright,
Lucid beginnings, casting doubts into flight.

Nocturne's Farewell

The moonlight fades, a silver frown,
Behind the veil of dawn's first light.
Stars retreat, the sky turns brown,
   Ushering in the end of night.

Dreams dissolve in morning's glance,
   Whispers of the dark now pass.
Silent fields in sunlight dance,
Transience held in cosmic glass.

Eclipses shadow night's domain,
While twilight weaves its mystic tale.
Moments of the night's refrain,
   Echo softly, shadows pale.

Tender Release

In the hush of broken chains,
Freedom gently spreads its wings.
Pain subsides, relief remains,
Whispered hope in spirit sings.

Burdens lift in silent grace,
Feathers float where weight once pressed.
Every heartache finds its place,
Tender moments now caressed.

From the grip of sorrow's hold,
Liberation breathes anew.
In the warmth, once bitter cold,
Tender release renews its view.

Morning's Prelude

Dewdrops kiss the waking earth,
Light unfurls in golden streams.
Birdsong heralds morning's birth,
Nature stirs from twilight dreams.

Horizon blushes, soft and meek,
Shadows flee from day's embrace.
Vibrant hues of daybreak speak,
Heralding the dawn's new grace.

Winds of dawn in whispers play,
Harmonizing with the morn.
Sunlight paints the skies to sway,
Prelude to a day reborn.

Tranquil Breaths

In the quiet, moments still,
Softly, silence holds its sway.
Peaceful breaths the air to fill,
Echoes of a tranquil day.

Ripples in a silent pond,
Reflect calm of skies so clear.
Nature's hand and heart respond,
Whispers only we can hear.

Serenity in gentle light,
Calm and grace in simple sights.
Tranquil breaths, both day and night,
Cradle hearts in soft delights.

Subdued Awakening

In the hush of early morn,
Dreams begin to fray,
Whispers of the waking light,
Guide the night away.

Soft hues of dawn emerge,
Painting skies serene,
Silent echoes of the stars,
Linger, yet unseen.

A breath of cool, crisp air,
Gently nudges sleep,
Nature's quiet lullaby,
In whispers, oh so deep.

Embers of the twilight,
Fade to pale, soft gold,
The world begins to stir anew,
A story yet untold.

In this peaceful stillness,
Life begins to bloom,
A subdued awakening,
From night's tender womb.

Harmony Rising

In the heart of morning's grace,
Melodies are born,
Echoes of a silent night,
Dissolving with the dawn.

Birds in chorus greet the sun,
With wings of pure delight,
Nature's symphony arises,
To end the tranquil night.

Each note a thread of unity,
Weaving day from night,
Harmony in every call,
A dance of sound and light.

The world awakens gently,
To rhythm and to rhyme,
Harmony is rising now,
In perfect, peaceful time.

In this concert of the dawn,
Hearts and souls unite,
Drawn to harmony's embrace,
In morning's tender light.

Dawn's Silence

In the stillness of early light,
A world in quiet keeps,
Soft sighs of dawn embracing night,
As shadows gently creep.

Morning's hush a whispered tale,
Of dreams that softly fade,
Clouds drift by in silent sail,
The night and day evade.

The air is calm, the earth serene,
As colors start to blend,
A canvas painted in between,
Where time and space transcend.

The silence sings a sacred song,
A hymn of peace and grace,
In dawn's embrace, we all belong,
Within this quiet space.

As light begins its slow ascent,
The silence holds us near,
In dawn's silence our hearts are sent,
To greet the day sincere.

Gentle Horizons

Upon the edge of morning,
Where night and day align,
A gentle sigh of dawning,
Unfurls in subtle sign.

Horizons bathed in tenderness,
Soft hues of pink and blue,
The sky in quieted bless,
Awaits the rising view.

Whispers of the night recede,
Beneath the light's caress,
Awakening in gentle deed,
A world in calm impress.

With each new ray that stretches far,
A promise softly spoken,
In light we read the morning's star,
New dawn now awoken.

Embrace the gentle horizon,
Where dreams and day converge,
In every dawn, new hope is rising,
And life begins to surge.

Slumber's End

As night's deep blanket slowly fades,
The dawn arrives in gentle shades.
Soft whispers in the morning air,
Brush freely with a tender care.

Shadows yield to day's first light,
Birds awake to grace the sky.
Our dreams release their fleeting hold,
As morning's arms around us fold.

Awake, awake, the world calls out,
Inviting all to shake their doubt.
In slumber's end, a promise new,
A day awaits, just out of view.

Delicate Uprising

A petal's dance in morning breeze,
So gentle, yet it brings unease.
A soft revolt beneath the sun,
As nature's song has just begun.

With quiet strength, the earth renews,
In silent bursts of varied hues.
Each tiny bloom, a subtle sign,
Of life's brave march, in line by line.

From roots unseen, they press ahead,
In delicate, unyielding tread.
To rise and greet the sky above,
A subtle force, a silent love.

Matinal Stillness

The world awaits in calm repose,
As dawn's first light in silence grows.
Not a stir disturbs the scene,
In matinal stillness, pure and serene.

The quiet hum of life's first breath,
Awakening from night's sweet death.
Each moment draped in fragile sound,
In morning's grace, where peace is found.

A symphony of silent hues,
Where day awakes and night subdues.
In stillness pure, our hearts align,
With nature's silent, sacred sign.

Quietude Arising

In morning's light, the quiet stirs,
A hush that speaks without words.
From the depth of night withdraws,
New day's breath in gentle cause.

A peace that sings in silent chords,
As dawn dispels night's final lords.
Each ray a whisper, soft and true,
Awakens life in shades of blue.

In quietude, the world imbibes,
A moment's pause, where stillness thrives.
As day ascends in silent cheer,
A rising calm to conquer fear.

Soft Horizons of Dawn

Whispers of light greet the morn,
Gently breaking night's embrace.
Colors bloom where dreams are born,
Brushstrokes soft, a quiet grace.

Morning mist begins to wane,
Shadows dance and start to play.
Earth awakens, free from chain,
Soft horizons lead the way.

Birdsong floats through silver air,
Nature hums a sweet refrain.
Hopes arise without a care,
In dawn's tender, warm domain.

Golden hues caress the land,
Warmth that spreads and soothes the soul.
Peace is held in morning's hand,
Soft horizons make us whole.

Promises of light remain,
Infinite, as skies unfold.
In the dawn, we break our chain,
Chasing dreams, the brave and bold.

The Soft Unveiling

Veils of night, softly lifting,
Revealing colors, gentle dawn.
Silence melts, dreams are sifting,
Nighttime shadows pale and drawn.

Pastel skies begin to brighten,
Bringing warmth, dispelling cold.
Morning stars start to enlighten,
Stories new and tales untold.

Flowers wake in morning's blush,
Petals kissed by tender light.
In this calm, there's no rush,
Day emerges from the night.

Soft unveiling, fresh and pure,
Promises born in new light.
World reborn, as dreams endure,
Held within the dawn's first sight.

Morning's grace, a fleeting touch,
Still, its glow remains so real.
Hearts will heal and hope as such,
Beneath dawn's soft, bright appeal.

Gentle Break of Day

In the quiet, soft and still,
Morning's light begins to play.
Glimmering o'er the distant hill,
Heralding the break of day.

Gentle hues of pink and gold,
Paint the sky with tender care.
In this light, the brave and bold,
Find their way through morning air.

Dew-kissed leaves in silent song,
Whisper tales of night's retreat.
In the dawn, we're pulled along,
Into light so pure and sweet.

Birds awake and start to sing,
Melodies of hope and cheer.
In the dawn, new dreams take wing,
Greeting daybreak with no fear.

Gentle break of day, you bring,
Softest touch to heart and soul.
In your light, we find our spring,
Breaking free to find our goal.

Dawn's Quiet Touch

In the stillness of first light,
Morning breaks with gentle grace.
Silver threads dispel the night,
Casting warmth on every face.

Silent whispers ride the breeze,
Morning's promise softly calls.
Through the branches of the trees,
Sunrise spreads its golden thralls.

Quiet touch of dawn's embrace,
Eases hearts and soothes the mind.
In the glow, we find our place,
Leaving shadowed thoughts behind.

Nature stirs, a symphony,
Notes that hum through morning's rise.
In the quiet, we are free,
Under soft and endless skies.

Dawn's sweet touch, a tender cure,
For the weary and the lost.
In its glow, we rest assured,
Finding peace at little cost.

Soft Birth

In silence, dawn unfurls anew,
A gentle breath, the world awake.
Light whispers through the morning dew,
A tender glow, the night's mistake.

Petals part to greet the day,
Soft pastels paint the waking skies.
In this quiet, shadows play,
With each heartbeat, the sunrise sighs.

Nature's hush, a sacred hymn,
New life stirs in each still sound.
Hope arises on a whim,
In this soft birth, all dreams are found.

Ripples in Time

A pebble falls in waters deep,
Circles spread in silent dance.
Moments weave through time's mystique,
Echoes cast in fleeting trance.

Yesterday's whispers, gentle breeze,
Kisses found in autumn's air.
Each ripple whispers, memories,
Fragments caught in time's care.

Seasons shift in endless flow,
Tides embrace the sands of fate.
Lives converge and gently grow,
In ripples, love perpetuates.

Morning's Coalesce

Morning breaks in hues of gold,
Dreams dissolve in light's caress.
Waking hearts, in warmth enfold,
Embrace the dawn, a sacred mess.

Shadows dance with waking light,
Night's embrace now gently fades.
Whispers of the coming fight,
In morning's coalesce, we wade.

New beginnings softly tread,
Life anew begins its quest.
Daylight calls on paths ahead,
Embrace today, in morning's zest.

Luminous Rebirth

From darkness, light begins to creep,
A spark ignites the weary heart.
In shadows' depths, where dreams may sleep,
Awakening, a brand new start.

Luminescent beams unfold,
Chasing night's embrace away.
Life in hues of molten gold,
Heralding a brighter day.

Reborn in light's eternal blaze,
Soul takes flight on wings so pure.
In this luminous, endless craze,
Find the strength in dawn's allure.

Dreamy Dawn

Whispers of the morning rise,
Golden hues in sleepy skies,
Stars diminish, shadows play,
Welcoming a brand new day.

Mist on valleys gently glides,
Birds awaken, newfound tides,
Nature's brushstroke, soft and wide,
Painting dreams for us to bide.

Cool breeze whispers through the pine,
Lover's kiss both sweet and fine,
Silent moments held in awe,
Dreamy dawn without a flaw.

Crimson streaks and amber shades,
Night's deep cloak in daylight fades,
Promises of what's to come,
Through the morning's gentle hum.

Restful Currents

Ripples dance on water's face,
Moonlight's shimmer, silent grace,
Softly swayed by evening breeze,
Calm beside the ancient trees.

Voices of the past reside,
In the depths where secrets hide,
Gentle currents soothe the mind,
Answers in their flow we find.

Pebbles whisper tales untold,
Of the river's journey bold,
Nature's verses softly speak,
In the currents, tender, meek.

Night descends with velvet touch,
Hold the peace within our clutch,
Drifting on in harmony,
Restful currents, wild and free.

Hushed Unfurling

Petals slowly come awake,
With the dawn, their thirst they slake,
Shade by shade, the blooms unfurl,
Silent whispers, nature's pearl.

Morning's breath on dewdrop fine,
Tracing patterns, pure, divine,
Every leaf a song unsung,
By the Earth's soft voice begun.

Colors blend in quiet weave,
Hushed as day prepares to eve,
Silent symphony in play,
Nature's art in soft display.

In the stillness, life unfolds,
Every moment, stories told,
Hushed unfurling, slow and true,
In each breath, the world anew.

Serenade of Daybreak

Softly sings the early bird,
Morning's call in whispers heard,
Melody of breaking day,
Guiding light along the way.

Sunrise casts a golden queue,
Sky awash in vibrant hue,
Echoes of a promise near,
Daybreak's serenade so clear.

Fields awake to morning's song,
Nature's chorus, pure and strong,
Harmony in every tone,
In this symphony we're shown.

Child of morning, bright and free,
Calls to hearts in melody,
Serenade of dawn's embrace,
Kissed by morning's gentle grace.

Day's Gentle Curve

In dawn's soft light, the world awakes,
Whispers of dreams the night forsakes.
Sunrise paints the morning sky,
A tender kiss as stars say goodbye.

Silent, the meadow's breeze does weave,
Songs of secrets leaves do cleave.
Nature's breath in harmony flows,
A tranquil start as daybreak grows.

Golden rays through curtains drift,
Gifting warmth in sunlight's lift.
Morning dew on petals gleam,
A new day's promise, an unspoken dream.

Shadow and light entwine with grace,
In life's serene and gentle pace.
Moments fleeting, tender, bright,
Unfolding softly in morning's light.

Harmony Embrace

Beneath the arch of twilight's gaze,
The earth and sky in colors blaze.
Hues of dusk in harmony blend,
As day and night together mend.

Echoes of life in evening's song,
Nature's voice both clear and strong.
Chirps and whispers in the breeze,
A symphony among the trees.

Stars emerge in velvet skies,
Glimmering where silence lies.
Moonlight dances on the sea,
Embracing night's tranquility.

Soft and tender moments steal,
A calm that hearts and souls can feel.
Harmony in every breath,
A fleeting peace where worries rest.

Veil of Morning

Morning's veil, so pure and light,
Lifts the darkness from the night.
Whispers of a new day's birth,
Spreading warmth across the earth.

Hues of amber, shades of gold,
Stories of the dawn unfold.
Each sunrise a gentle tale,
Hope and dreams within its trail.

Birds awaken, songs arise,
Melodies where silence lies.
Nature's choir greets the dawn,
In harmonious, gentle yawn.

Daylight's reach, a tender sweep,
Stirring life from restful sleep.
Promises in sun's first ray,
A fresh beginning, a bright new day.

Muted Awakening

The morning stirs in muted tones,
Soft whispers as the daylight hones.
Shadows fade in slow retreat,
As sun unfolds the dawn's receipt.

Leaves rustle in a gentle breeze,
Nature's fingers through the trees.
Soft light dapples, kisses earth,
A quiet tune of morning's mirth.

Mist rises from the slumbering ground,
Silent, yet with presence found.
Awakening in subtle hue,
A palette fresh, serene, and new.

Day unfolds in calm embrace,
A tender start, a measured pace.
Muted whispers, softly clear,
Morning's breath so calm and near.

Dawning Tranquility

The sky awakes in hues so light,
Night's blanket lifts, yields to sight.
Stars fade gently, dawn arrests,
Nature's canvas slowly rests.

Whispers of the morning dew,
Tell a tale, old yet new.
Fields embrace the tender day,
Silence speaks in calm array.

Birdsongs thread through silent air,
Melodies delicate, rare.
Petals stretch to greet the morn,
Life renews, dreams reborn.

Stillness cradles the first ray,
Promising a hopeful day.
Every breath, a fresh delight,
In the dawning, pure and bright.

Shadows yield to soft embrace,
Day unfolds with gentle grace.
Peace descends in golden streams,
Dawning tranquility redeems.

Whispering Sunlight

Golden beams through curtains slip,
Morning's kiss on lips of sleep.
Dreams dissolve in warming light,
Whispers of a day so bright.

Leaves converse in sunlight glows,
Breezes hum through quiet rows.
Nature's secrets softly told,
In the warmth of buzzing gold.

Meadows blush in soft embrace,
Sunlight paints a tender face.
Glistening dew on blades of grass,
Sparkles like a crystal glass.

Shadows dance in light's soft play,
Chasing night and birthing day.
Every hue a story weaves,
Whispering in sunlit leaves.

Rippling streams reflect the glow,
Joyful currents gently flow.
Nature's voice in sun's sweet gleam,
Whispering dreams in golden beam.

Mellow Rise

Morning breathes with gentle ease,
Day unfolds with tender breeze.
Soft hues chase the night away,
Mellow tones in break of day.

Clouds disperse in pastel cheer,
Sun ascends, bright and clear.
Birdsong fills the waking skies,
Harmony as dawn arise.

Golden touches on the ground,
Silence wears a soothing sound.
Every sight a soft surprise,
In the early mellow rise.

Shadows fade in light's embrace,
Stillness cloaked in gentle grace.
Moments linger, soft and kind,
Peace found in the morning's mind.

Nature's symphony begins,
Dewdrops dance on leaf and skin.
Daylight blooms in gentle flight,
Mellow rise in warm delight.

Still Waters Ascend

Mirror of the morning skies,
Waters calm as day implies.
Reflections in stillness blend,
Nature's echoes to ascend.

Ripples whisper on the lake,
Tranquil hum, no sound to break.
Every wave a lullaby,
Kissing shores with gentle sigh.

Sunlight's path on water weaves,
Glowing trails through quiet leaves.
Shimmering in golden threads,
Through the hearts of flow it spreads.

Calmness cradles every crest,
Bringing stillness to its best.
Harmony in every bend,
Still waters with grace ascend.

Glistening in morning's glow,
Soft as feathers, calm as snow.
Life in peaceful moments penned,
Still waters gently ascend.

Beneath Still Mornings

In the hush of dawning light,
Whispers of the night take flight,
Silence wraps the world with care,
Breathing peace into the air.

Shadows fade in gentle sweep,
Waking dreams from endless sleep,
Birdsongs stir the tranquil breeze,
Rustling leaves in ancient trees.

Dewdrops kiss the meadow green,
Glittering gems, a sight unseen,
Nature's canvas softly drawn,
Welcomes in the break of dawn.

Mountains watch with granite eyes,
Guardians of the morning skies,
Rivers hum a tender tune,
Flowing under sun and moon.

Moments linger, pure and bright,
Spirits rise with newfound might,
Beneath still mornings, hope is born,
Promising a world reborn.

Soft Sun's Emergence

Golden beams through windows creep,
Stirring life from gentle sleep,
Whispers weave through morning air,
Delicate beyond compare.

Petals turn to greet the light,
Chasing shadows from the night,
Every hue in vibrant play,
Heralds in another day.

Tender rays caress the earth,
Marking moments of rebirth,
Sky adorned in pastel shades,
Softening the night's charades.

Murmurs of a waking land,
Harmony at nature's hand,
Soft sun's emergence blesses all,
Answering the dawn's soft call.

Hearts align with whispered prayer,
Finding solace unaware,
In the glow of morning's grace,
We embrace a sweet embrace.

Tranquility's Unfolding

Morning mist on silent lakes,
Calm as breath that gently takes,
Fading dreams in twilight's hold,
Stories of the night retold.

Echoes of the dawn arise,
Soft as wings of butterflies,
Harmony in nature's song,
Guides the heart to where it belongs.

Lightest touch of morning's hand,
Paints a portrait vast and grand,
Every line and shade aligns,
Crafting peace in fine designs.

Stillness wraps the waking world,
Like a flag of hope unfurled,
Moments drift on tender sighs,
Borne on breezes, pure and wise.

Tranquility unfolds with ease,
In the dance of rustling trees,
Through the symphony of day,
Leading hearts along its way.

Graceful Dawn

Touched by light in whispered hue,
Morning bids the night adieu,
Graceful dawn in softest rise,
Paints its story in the skies.

Hills and valleys bathed in gold,
Silent tales of love retold,
Streams reflect the heavens' glow,
In their gentle, onward flow.

Stars relinquish to the sun,
Knowing day has just begun,
Brilliant hues of pink and blue,
Celebrate the morning dew.

Whispers felt in every breath,
Life renewed from nightly death,
Graceful dawn bestows its kiss,
In a moment's perfect bliss.

As the sun ascends its throne,
All the world's with warmth aglow,
Hearts rejoice in light's embrace,
Greeting dawn with simple grace.

Stillness in Bloom

A petal falls in quiet grace,
Whispers to the morning dew.
In stillness, nature finds its place,
Where moments pause and skies are true.

The breeze conveys a soft hello,
To leaves that shimmer, green and bright.
In silence, streams of beauty flow,
Each blossom bathes in golden light.

A butterfly with gentle wings,
Brushes past the waiting rose.
In the garden, courage springs,
Peaceful pathways life bestows.

Sunbeams dance amid the leaves,
Casting shadows, pure and sweet.
In this stillness, no one grieves,
Stillness brings the heart to beat.

Flowers stand in soft array,
Silent witnesses of time.
In their peace, the hopes convey,
Joy within this tranquil rhyme.

Peaceful Emergence

Morning mist on meadows lay,
Softly fades as dawn appears.
In this light, the dreams relay,
Whispers of forgotten years.

Birds begin their gentle song,
Melody that clears the mind.
In their notes, where souls belong,
Peace and love, forever twined.

A new day breaks, and hearts arise,
From the earth, a gentle sigh.
In the warmth of morning skies,
Hope and grace begin to fly.

Silent rivers start to flow,
Gathering the night's embrace.
In each ripple, love will grow,
Echoes of a calm, safe space.

With each breath, a world renewed,
Gentle hearts, in unison.
With the morning, faith is cued,
Peaceful springs, where life is spun.

Quiet Horizons

The distant hills in twilight hue,
Whisper secrets, calm and old.
Beyond the skies, in depths of blue,
Stories of the world unfold.

An evening breeze that gently sighs,
Carries dreams across the land.
In horizons, quiet lies,
Moments poised by nature's hand.

Stars emerge in silent grace,
Lighting paths of still unknown.
In this quiet, we embrace,
Horizons where our hearts have flown.

Calm waters meet the endless shore,
Reflecting peace, a silver glow.
In the silence, hear the lore,
Of places where the night winds blow.

As dusk gives way to night serene,
Whispers echo, soft and mild.
In the quiet, spirits glean,
Horizons where dreams run wild.

Dawn's Embrace

The dawn breaks with a tender kiss,
Chasing shadows from the night.
In its light, we find our bliss,
Hopes reborn in morning's sight.

The world awakens, fresh and new,
With colors vivid, pure and bright.
In this dawn, our dreams renew,
Hearts prepared for love's invite.

Mountains greet the rising sun,
Bathe in warmth, and stand with pride.
In this embrace, the day's begun,
Journeys where the spirits ride.

Whispers of the morning breeze,
Gently brush the waking earth.
In its song, the soul finds ease,
Moments filled with joy and mirth.

With each ray, the heart does swell,
Bound by light, in dawn's embrace.
In this glow, all fears dispel,
Life's new chapter, full of grace.

Morning Serenity

The dawn breaks with tender light,
Kissing the dew-kissed earth,
Whispers of dreams make flight,
In the gentle morning's birth.

The world awakens in hues of gold,
Silent moments soft and sweet,
Nature's tales as yet untold,
In the daybreak's calm heartbeat.

Birds sing soft, a chorus bright,
Melodies of peace and grace,
Breezes cool in the clear skylight,
Caressing earth's gentle face.

Flowers stretch with graceful sighs,
Towards the sun's warm embrace,
Morning rays in soft replies,
Cast a glow on nature's space.

In this time of pure delight,
Harmony and peace unite,
Morning's serenity in sight,
A tranquil, exquisite rite.

The Soft Echo of Morn

Whispers of dawn in the stillness,
As night's embrace slowly wanes,
A soft gleam, pure and illness,
Banishes stars' faint remains.

Morning breathes in quiet sighs,
Casting dreams upon the wind,
Awakening with tender eyes,
New tales that day might spin.

Each moment as the light springs,
Carries echoes soft and meek,
The silent songs the dawn brings,
Words tender yet unique.

In the hush of morning's glow,
The world's pulse, steady, slow,
A ballet in the heavens' show,
In dawn's soft, gentle flow.

As the sun ascends the sky,
A canvas painted bright and spry,
The morning's echo whispers why,
In peace, our spirits fly.

Beneath Quiet Skies

Beneath the skies so calm and gray,
Morning whispers softly start,
Every cloud keeps night at bay,
As dawn enchants the heart.

The lakes reflect a tranquil sheen,
Mirrors to the sky's embrace,
Beneath the tendrils of sun's sheen,
Nature's quiet, gentle grace.

Each leaf rustles a tender song,
In the breezes cool and light,
Morn's embrace, where we all belong,
Soft as the twilight's flight.

In fields of whispered memories,
The grasses sway, the flowers beam,
Underneath the quiet seas,
Of the morning's lucid dream.

Beneath the skies so calm and kind,
Peace and joy in the heart we'll find,
In these moments, our souls unwind,
Morning's gentle worlds aligned.

Tranquil Morning Hues

The morn arrives in subtle hues,
Soft pastels of light and shade,
In the mist, the world renews,
A serene dawn gently made.

The colors blend in harmony,
A dance upon the canvas wide,
Moments of infinity,
Where soft serenity resides.

Each hue, a whisper, kind and true,
A gentle brush of morning's kiss,
A blanket woven in soft blue,
Of silent, calming bliss.

The day unfolds in painted light,
In shades of gold and muted glare,
As nature's hand crafts pure delight,
In the tranquil morning air.

These tranquil morning hues bestow,
A soothing peace, a tender glow,
In these moments, spirits grow,
As dawn sets hearts aglow.

Whispering Morn

The dawn awakes in hues of gold,
Soft murmurs through the skies unfold.
The world in tender light adorned,
A new day fluidly reborn.

With whispers soft the breezes talk,
Among the dew-kissed fields they walk.
Each leaf a song, each branch a chord,
In whispered morn, all hearts are soared.

Voices blend with gentle sighs,
In early light, where silence lies.
A moment caught 'twixt night and day,
Where dreams and hopes together play.

The morning whispers secrets new,
Of skies in pink and oceans blue.
In every chirp, in every call,
The morning's whisper reaches all.

Awakened now, the world revolves,
In whispered morn, all resolves.
With light and love, a tranquil scorn,
The day begins, a beauty sworn.

Stillness Borne

In the quiet of the night,
Stars above in mystic flight.
A stillness borne from realms afar,
Kisses the earth like a fallen star.

Silent whispers through the air,
Moments caught in gentle care.
A hush that births a tender calm,
Cradles the heart in a soothing psalm.

Stillness wraps with velvet touch,
A cloak that mutes the world's clutch.
In soft embrace, the soul is found,
In stillness borne, love is crowned.

The night bestows its silent grace,
Upon the world, a quiet place.
In every breath, in every sigh,
A stillness borne beneath the sky.

The stillness holds a secret note,
In silence, truth begins to float.
With peace infused, the night transforms,
A symphony in quiet forms.

Gentle Radiance

In gentle beams, the sunlight falls,
Through verdant leaves and ancient walls.
A radiance soft, and pure, and bright,
Illuminates the day and night.

The morning's touch, a golden hue,
In every drop of morning dew.
A gentle radiance, so serene,
Caresses all in light's soft sheen.

The flowers bloom in radiant cheer,
Their colors dance to light so clear.
In every petal, in every face,
A gentle radiance shows its grace.

With every wave, the oceans glow,
Beneath the sun's warm, tender flow.
In every glimmer, in every glance,
A gentle light in sweet romance.

The world, it basks in softest fire,
A light that never seems to tire.
In gentle radiance, hearts align,
A touch of heaven, so divine.

Heavenly Murmur

The skies above in azure blue,
Whisper secrets old and new.
A heavenly murmur through the air,
Weaves a dream, beyond compare.

Clouds drift by on silken waves,
In celestial dance, the heart behaves.
A murmur soft from heaven's choir,
Ignites the soul with gentle fire.

The stars at night, in twinkling grace,
Murmur tales from time and space.
Each cosmic note, a song so fine,
Echoes in the grand design.

The moonlight casts a silver beam,
In heavenly murmur, a tranquil dream.
Through night it sings, a lullaby,
That cradles hearts beneath the sky.

In every breath, in every sound,
A heavenly murmur all around.
Soft as whispers, yet profound,
In murmur's veil, peace is found.

Mellow Dawn's Kiss

Whispers of light through trees they weave,
Softly the morning starts to breathe,
A dew-kissed world begins to wake,
With each bright ray, the shadows break.

The sky blushes with hues of gold,
As stories of the night unfold,
Birds sing melodies of bliss,
Inspired by the dawn's first kiss.

Mountains stand and waters flow,
Lit by the morning's tender glow,
Where night once reigned, the sun now shines,
Painting dreams in soft, sweet lines.

In tranquil fields where flowers sway,
Embracing warmly, the new day,
With every light, a promise made,
To chase the dark with the sun's parade.

Beneath the calm of morning's mist,
We greet the day with hearts unmissed,
Thankful for the gentle start,
Of mellow dawn's sweet, tender art.

Awakening Tranquility

The silence sings in morning's grace,
A peaceful heart in nature's place,
Soft whispers of a waking land,
Held tenderly by dawn's own hand.

Dewdrops glisten on leaves so green,
Reflecting skies, serene unseen,
Breeze caresses with gentle sighs,
As light first touches sleepy eyes.

In quiet moments, breath restored,
A world reborn without a sword,
The magic lies in daybreak's view,
A canvas painted fresh and new.

Echoes of the night now fade,
A new day's sleep serene cascade,
Tranquility in every hue,
Morning lights that break anew.

In dawn's embrace, we find our peace,
Where hurried thoughts begin to cease,
Awakening to softest light,
Guided gently by dawn's flight.

First Light's Lullaby

At horizon's edge where stars depart,
First light whispers to the heart,
A song of dawn sung soft and sweet,
To lull the world from its retreat.

Crimson streaks that paint the morn,
From night's cocoon, a new day's born,
A lullaby that eases night,
Into the arms of warming light.

With feathered notes, the birds convene,
To harmonize a waking scene,
Melodies of light that play,
As darkness gently slips away.

In morning's hymn, the soul finds rest,
Peace in sunlight manifest,
A gentle nudge to rise and shine,
With daybreak's tune, our hearts align.

Ethereal chords in sky's embrace,
Morning's song in perfect grace,
To greet the day with open eyes,
Led softly by first light's lullabies.

Daylight's Gentle Rise

Morning spreads its golden hue,
Casting dreams in shades anew,
The gentle rise of daylight's kiss,
Awakens earth with tender bliss.

Fields bathed in softest amber light,
Promises of day so bright,
Every shadow takes its leave,
As dawn's first rays begin to weave.

Silhouettes in light's embrace,
Every line, a touch of grace,
Nature stirs and life renews,
Bathed in countless golden hues.

Birds take flight in sky's expanse,
In daylight's glow, they gaily dance,
Welcoming the warmth that spreads,
Across the world from sunlit heads.

With tender rays and softest rise,
Daylight opens sleeping eyes,
A world reborn in morn's fresh guise,
Embracing all 'neath open skies.

Soft Illumination

Within the pale moon's gentle glow,
Where whispers of twilight softly flow,
A world of dreams begins to show,
In hues of silver, soft and slow.

The stars above, a scattered light,
Guide travelers through the quiet night,
Their shimmering paths, pure and bright,
Illuminate the dark with gentle might.

With every breath of cool, calm air,
A sense of stillness fills the lair,
A tranquil haven, free from care,
Embraced by moonbeams, rare and fair.

The shadows dance on fields of green,
Their patterns cast a mystic sheen,
In this serene and peaceful scene,
A tranquil reverie, serene.

The dawn will come with golden rays,
But for now, in this quiet phase,
We bask in night's soft, peaceful blaze,
In moonlit dreams, our hearts shall gaze.

Subtle Radiance

Beneath the sky's vast canopy,
Where sunlight glows so tenderly,
A subtle radiance, wild and free,
   Whispers secrets of the sea.

The morning mist, with gentle grace,
   Caresses softly every place,
A silken veil, with light to trace,
The contours of the earth's embrace.

In meadows where the flowers sway,
Each petal touched by dawn's first ray,
   A dance of light begins to play,
And colors bloom in bright array.

The river's flow, a gentle stream,
Reflects the sun's elusive gleam,
In every ripple's fleeting beam,
A tranquil, soft, and golden dream.

As day unfolds, the shadows wane,
With light's soft touch in every lane,
   A harmony of joy and pain,
In subtle radiance, we remain.

Restful Mornings

In restful mornings, soft and still,
The world awakens, temperate and chill,
With whispers of the waking hill,
And dawn's embrace, a gentle thrill.

The first light breaks through shades of night,
A tender touch, so calm and light,
In golden hues, the sky's delight,
Unfolds anew, a pure sight.

Birds serenade the rising day,
Their melodies in soft array,
A chorus in the morning's play,
Welcoming the sun's first ray.

The air is crisp, the breeze is kind,
A tranquil peace, in day we find,
With gentle whispers in the mind,
And morning's grace, our hearts unwind.

In restful mornings, free from haste,
We find our souls in quiet place,
Embracing moments, pure and chaste,
In dawn's soft glow, a tender grace.

Serene Rebirth

At dawn's first light, the world renews,
In shades of soft, reflective hues,
A serene rebirth, where dreams infuse,
With morning's breath, the earth reviews.

The dew that clings to blades of grass,
A fleeting kiss, as shadows pass,
In nature's mirror, clear as glass,
We see the promise, bold and vast.

The flowers bloom with colors bright,
In fields awash with morning light,
A tapestry, serene and right,
Unfolds beneath the sky's delight.

Each day begins with hope anew,
In every drop of morning dew,
A world reborn in every view,
With skies of gold and clouds of blue.

In moments still, we find our grace,
In nature's calm and warm embrace,
A serene rebirth, in time and space,
Where hope and peace find their place.

Quiet Dawn Reflections

The sky with hues so tender, calm,
Whispers start the day anew,
Nature's brush, a timeless balm,
Softly paints the morning dew.

In the stillness, thoughts align,
Dreams unweave their silent thread,
Waking hours, moments fine,
Soft reflections gently spread.

Birdsong breaks the fragile mist,
Notes of hope and peace they send,
Day's first light by breezes kissed,
In tranquility, they blend.

Shadows dance on morning's stage,
Sunlight peeks with gentle grace,
Each new dawn, another page,
In life's story, finds its place.

Peace in silence fondly grows,
Morning's gift, a quiet plea,
Cherish now, the world bestows,
Moments caught in reverie.

Soft Day's Birth

Gentle whispers greet the morn,
Light spills soft on fields of green,
Day's new chapter, freshly born,
In the quiet, all is seen.

Morning breaks with subtle glow,
Nature stirs from restful sleep,
Warm hues touch the earth below,
Silent vows the sunrise keeps.

Softly does the world arise,
In the stillness, hearts embrace,
Day blooms under tranquil skies,
Radiance fills every space.

New beginnings grace the land,
As the shadows fade away,
Life awakes, a gentle hand,
Guiding light to start the day.

Delicate as morning mist,
Dawn's first light reveals the birth,
In the calm, by sunbeams kissed,
Softest dawn adorns the earth.

First Rays of Quiet

First rays pierce the evening's shroud,
Whispers brush the silent hills,
Night recedes, the sky is proud,
Morning's glow, the heart it fills.

Nature wakes with gentle grace,
Songs of birds float on the breeze,
Light's first touch, a warm embrace,
Lost in moments such as these.

Stillness sits upon the ground,
Soft reflections in the dew,
Magic in the dawn is found,
In each day, a promise new.

Shades of gold and blush arise,
Tinting clouds with tender hue,
Morning opens sleepy eyes,
Dreams and hopes are born anew.

Quiet lingers, moments sweet,
As the world in light is dressed,
In the silence, hearts will meet,
Morning's call to rise and bless.

Subtle Dawn Awakening

In the hush of breaking dawn,
Light creeps in on resting plains,
Day's first breath, a gentle yawn,
Tender touch of sunlight reigns.

Shadows lift and fade away,
Morning stirs with peaceful grace,
Sky adorned in soft array,
Light illuminates the space.

Whispers float on cool, crisp air,
Dreams dissolve as day begins,
Nature's beauty, always fair,
Wakes in harmony, she spins.

Golden hues caress the land,
Life revives from slumber's deep,
In this quiet, calm is planned,
Secrets of the dawn to keep.

Morning's tender, patient rise,
Greets the world with calm embrace,
In its light, the spirit flies,
Softly dawn's new promises place.

Quiet Unveiling

In the hush of morning's grace,
Whispers dance upon the leaves,
Distilled moments found a place,
Where time, a gentle web weaves.

Petals bloom in silent cheer,
Soft hues wake the dormant day,
Nature's breath is calm yet clear,
Anchoring the light to stay.

A sparrow's song breaks the peace,
Stitching stories with its call,
Each note bids the night to cease,
In this tranquil, tender sprawl.

River's edge, where shadows flit,
Ripples sketch the dawn's first gleam,
Every wave a poem writ,
Reflecting life, a waking dream.

Eyes that meet the dawn anew,
Catch the echo of a sigh,
In the quiet unveiling, true,
The world lifts its sleepy eye.

Awakening Echos

Morning winds through night's last breath,
Bringing echoes from afar,
Ghostly whispers, tales of death,
Songs beneath the morning star.

Mountains hum with ancient lore,
Valleys sigh a waking hymn,
Nature's pulses speak once more,
In a symphony so dim.

Echoes weave the breaking morn,
Threads of light and shadow blend,
In their dance, new hope is born,
Each reverberation's end.

Sounds of life, a gentle rise,
From the deep, old chords ascend,
Whispers morph to joyful cries,
In this chorus, voices mend.

Awakening, the world renews,
Echos fade and then take flight,
In serene, reflective hues,
Sound and light merge to unite.

Pensive Sunrise

Sunlight creeps through fragile skies,
Breaking dawn with tender flames,
In the morning's soft reprise,
Life reclaims its silent frames.

Shadows long and dreams unfold,
Night's embrace begins to wane,
In the glow, reflections hold,
Every tear and every strain.

Contemplation fills the air,
Thoughts like dew on petals cling,
Moments caught in morning's glare,
Reflect the hopes they gently bring.

Wisps of clouds, a painter's brush,
Stroke the sky in hues of gold,
In the quiet, gentle hush,
Stories of the heart unfold.

Eyes that seek the rising dawn,
Find a world both old and new,
In this pensive hour's spawn,
Dreams awake, renewed by view.

Melancholy Light

Dusk descends with somber grace,
Hues of twilight paint the land,
In the veil of night's embrace,
Lonely shadows softly stand.

Whispers lost in evening's breeze,
Carry tales of distant shores,
Echoes of forgotten pleas,
Murmur through the closing doors.

Stars, like tears in velvet sky,
Glint with silent, distant cries,
In their glow, memories lie,
Mirroring the heart's goodbyes.

Melancholy light descends,
Casting doubts and fading dreams,
Time, it flows and never bends,
Through the silvery moonlit streams.

Eyes that linger in the dark,
Searching constellations bright,
Find within the shadowed arc,
Fragments of the fading light.

Whispers of Day

The morning dew, in silence lay,
Upon the grass, where memories play.
Sunrise whispers soft and kind,
A gentle touch upon the mind.

Birdsongs break the night's embrace,
With melodies that fill the space.
Shadows fade as light prevails,
In this dance of cosmic tales.

A whisper here, a murmur there,
Nature's secrets fill the air.
Each leaf, each breeze, a story spun,
In the whispers of the dawn begun.

Mountains stand in quiet grace,
Guardians of this tranquil place.
Valleys echo with the day,
As night's whispers fade away.

In the stillness of this hour,
Daybreak blooms, a fragile flower.
Whispers of the day unfold,
A tapestry of light and gold.

Eloquent Morn

The sky awakens with a sigh,
Colours blush in striking dye.
Morning's grace, an artist's dream,
In the soft horizon's gleam.

Echoes of a night now past,
In the light, our shadows cast.
Dreams dissolve in morning air,
Promises whispered everywhere.

Breezes play with strands of hair,
Sighs of dawn, without a care.
Whispers turn to nature's hum,
In the glow of morning's sum.

Every leaf and every tree,
Speaks in tones of mystery.
In the eloquence of dawn,
Nature's symphony is drawn.

Skies of blue and clouds awry,
In the morn, our spirits fly.
Hope and joy, the day adorn,
In the breath of eloquent morn.

Horizon's Caress

Where sky meets sea in soft caress,
A dance of endless tenderness.
Boundless realms of azure blend,
In the horizon's gentle bend.

Waves that kiss the sandy shore,
A symphony forevermore.
Whispers of the ocean's breath,
A lullaby in nature's depth.

Golden beam and twilight's trace,
Grace the horizon's warm embrace.
Heavens reach to touch the earth,
In this meeting, endless worth.

Clouds drift high, in silent grace,
Patterned in this wondrous space.
Each day ends, a promise kept,
Where horizon's dreams have slept.

Infinite the line that binds,
Nature's secrets, undefined.
In horizon's soft caress,
Lies our earthly tenderness.

Blushing Meadows

Fields awash in twilight's blush,
A world of calm, devoid of rush.
Petals whisper in the breeze,
In the glow of gentle ease.

Blossoms painted by the sun,
As the day is nearly done.
Golden hues and pastel skies,
In the meadow, beauty lies.

Every flower, every blade,
In nature's palette softly laid.
Blushing under heaven's light,
Turning day into the night.

Crickets hum a serenade,
As daylight's colours gently fade.
Nature sings its soft goodbyes,
In the fields 'neath darkening skies.

Meadows blush in warm embrace,
As stars begin their nightly chase.
In the twilight's tender glow,
Blushing meadows softly know.

Morning's Gentle Embrace

The sun peeks through in golden grace,
Starting the day with a tender face.
Birds' songs fill the skies above,
Awakening the world with love.

Dewdrops glisten on the grass,
Moments of beauty that swiftly pass.
A breeze that whispers soft and low,
Morning's secrets in its flow.

Mountains blush in early light,
Chasing away the remnants of night.
Shadows stretch and slowly fade,
In the warmth of dawn's parade.

Children's laughter echoes near,
A joyful start, a voice so clear.
Mother Nature wears her gown,
In hues of amber, red, and brown.

In morning's gentle, warm embrace,
The world awakens with soft grace.
A promise of the day to come,
Under the sky's vast kingdom.

Silent Horizons

Beyond where sight begins to fade,
Lies the horizon, serenely made.
Whispers of the world's vast end,
In silent breaths, the colors blend.

Mountains cradled by the sky,
Telling tales of times gone by.
Valleys deep and rivers wide,
Secrets in the shadows hide.

The ocean's edge, a quiet line,
Where dreams and reality entwine.
Waves that kiss the sandy shore,
In silence, speak forevermore.

Whispers of the wind so cold,
Stories of the ages told.
Horizons stretch beyond our gaze,
Silent in their mystic ways.

Twilight brings a deeper hue,
Stars awaken in the blue.
Silent horizons, so profound,
In their quiet, wisdom found.

Whispers of Dawn

Light touches the horizon's seam,
A whisper of the dawn's first dream.
Soft pastels paint the morning sky,
As night-time's shadows bid goodbye.

Birds awaken with a song,
Heralding the day so long.
In the hush of dawn's first light,
Hope dispels the cloak of night.

Trees in silhouette stand tall,
Silent watchers of it all.
In the calm before the day,
Whispers of the dawn convey.

Cool air rests upon the land,
Soft whispers through the trees as planned.
Each breath a promise of renewal,
Dawn's embrace, gentle and so true.

As the world begins to wake,
Dawn's whispers dreams unmake.
A new day's light begins to spawn,
In the tender whispers of the dawn.

Serene Beginnings

Morning light that softly beams,
Awakens nature from its dreams.
A peace that hovers in the air,
Dawn's serenity laid bare.

Mist that dances with the breeze,
Through the branches of the trees.
A world reborn with each new sun,
Serene beginnings have begun.

Streams that murmur as they flow,
Secrets of the dawn they know.
Gentle ripples kiss the shore,
In their quiet, something more.

Fields that bask in morning's glow,
A canvas painted long and slow.
Flora wakes in hues of green,
Serene beginnings, fresh and clean.

Eyes that open to the day,
Hearts that find a gentle way.
With each dawn, the world renews,
In serene beginnings, life subdues.

Softly Glowing Horizons

The sky extends in pastel hues,
A gentle blend of dusk and dawn.
Whispers of dreams in twilight muse,
The night retreats, the day is born.

Mountains blush in morning's gaze,
Their peaks caressed by amber light.
A symphony of new-born days,
Guides the starry realms to night.

In the meadow, shadows flee,
Succumbing to the sun's embrace.
Softly glowing horizons see,
The dawn unveil her timeless grace.

Birdsong graces the moist air,
Melodies of joy and peace.
The world awakens void of care,
In nature's grand, unending piece.

Moments linger in the light,
Softly glowing—pure and wise.
Promises of wondrous sights,
Reflect in the morning's rise.

The Quiet Bloom

Beneath the gentle twilight's beam,
A quiet bloom begins her song.
Subtle scents in evening's dream,
Where shadows dance, and days prolong.

Petals unfurl with silent grace,
Whispers of life in every fold.
In stillness, beauty finds its place,
A tale of time and love retold.

In gardens where the night birds sing,
The quiet bloom of deep repose.
Her essence graced by moon's soft ring,
A star within the soil rose.

Soft winds carry tales anew,
Of gardens kissed by morning dew.
Each bud a notion, pure and true,
In silence, paths to grace construe.

Beneath the stars, the blooms abide,
Their gentle whispers undefined.
In nature's hush, they softly bide,
Their stories to the night confined.

Easing into Day

Morning light through curtains peeks,
Softly waking, world anew.
Easing into day's slight creaks,
Night's calm whispers bid adieu.

The air hangs cool with dew's embrace,
Each breath awash in nature's scent.
Sunrise paints the sky with grace,
A canvas where the dreams are spent.

Gentle steps in morning's hush,
Pathways kissed by dawn's first gleam.
Moments stretch, no need to rush,
Life unfolding in a dream.

Songs of birds, a choir unseen,
Harmonize the birth of light.
Easing into day's serene,
Leaving behind the veil of night.

With every dawn, new love ignites,
Majestic through its quiet sway.
In gold and amber, softly bright,
We find peace, easing into day.

Whispered Light

In the tender dawn's first glow,
Whispered light begins to creep.
Threads of gold, all things bestow,
Waking life from twilight's sleep.

Mountains shrouded in mist's veil,
Slowly breathe in morning's tune.
Whispered light in valleys trails,
Guiding shadows to commune.

Leaves with dew in silence churred,
Glimmer bright in whispered beams.
Nature's chorus, all transfused,
In this quiet dance of dreams.

The world in hush, awaits day's haste,
In every color's slow reveal.
Whispered light, with gentle grace,
Unveils the truths we subtly feel.

Soft and tender, daybreak's call,
Whispered light that warms the heart.
Ethereal glow that catches all,
In dawn's pure love, we never part.

www.ingramcontent.com/pod-product-compliance
Lightning Source LLC
LaVergne TN
LVHW010558070526
838199LV00063BA/5010